LET'S VISIT IRELAND

Let's visit
IRELAND

**PETER EADIE
AND
CYRIL DUFF**

BURKE

ACKNOWLEDGEMENTS

The authors and publishers are grateful to the following for permission to reproduce photographs in this book:

The Belfast Telegraph; J. Allan Cash; C. M. Dixon; Bill Doyle; Noeline Kelly; Irish Tourist Board; Keystone Press Agency Ltd.; Northern Ireland Ministry of Commerce and Northern Ireland Tourist Board.

The colour photograph on the cover is reproduced by permission of Odhams Press Syndication.

CIP data

Eadie, Peter
  Let's visit Ireland. – 4th ed.
  1. Ireland – Social life and customs – Juvenile literature
  I. Title   II. Duff, Cyril
  941.5082'4   DA925
ISBN 0 222 01022 3

Burke Publishing Company Limited
Pegasus House, 116–120 Golden Lane, London EC1Y 0TL, England.
Burke Publishing (Canada) Limited
Registered Office: 20 Queen Street West, Suite 3000, Box 30, Toronto, Canada M5H 1V5.
Burke Publishing Company Inc.
Registered Office: 333 State Street, PO Box 1740, Bridgeport, Connecticut 06601, U.S.A.
Filmset in "Monophoto" Baskerville by Green Gates Studios Ltd., Hull, England.
Printed in Singapore by Tien Wah Press (Pte.) Ltd.

Contents

The Story of Ireland

Ireland, the large island off the west coast of Britain, is on the fringe of the European land mass known as the "continental shelf". If the surface of the sea were slightly lowered, Ireland would become, along with Britain, part of the mainland of Europe which lies to the east. To the west of Ireland, the nearest land is on the other side of the Atlantic Ocean, hence the people of County Kerry frequently say that the next parish to theirs is in Boston, U.S.A.

Ireland's geographical position in Europe has made the country of special interest to the archaeologist. Because she is so far from Central Europe, and because the Romans did not invade her, much of her ancient history has been preserved, and remains have been found which give information about the wanderings of many pre-historic peoples.

The first people to come to Ireland were the Larnian race who lived in about 6000 B.C. They are believed to have come from southern France. They travelled northwards up the French Atlantic coast to Brittany, and from there sailed in their dug-out canoes across the Irish Sea to the north-east coast of Ireland.

They were small people who must have been excellent sailors; their canoes were frail craft and the Irish Sea is sometimes stormy. They lived simply—some of their simple tools have been found in recent years. They gathered berries, for food, and varied their diet by catching wild birds and fish

It is believed that some of their settlements were submerged when the level of the Irish Sea rose.

The first farmers came to Britain and Ireland in about 4000 B.C. They were small, slight, olive-skinned people from the Mediterranean area, with long heads, lean faces and narrow noses. They knew how to grow barley and wheat and how to keep domestic and farm animals. They stored their milk and grain in hand-made pottery.

During the period between 3500 B.C. and 1000 B.C. there was a further migration to Ireland and Britain of Mediterranean people. They are believed to have been tall, fair and blue-eyed. They built the giant tombs of the Stone Age. Some of these can still be seen today. On the River Boyne, just north of Dublin, for example, is Newgrange—one of the most magnificent burial mounds in the western world. These circular shrines or tombs include "dolmens" which were built by setting one great stone, known as a capstone, of tremendous weight, across the top of three or four great upright stones. To this day, no one knows how these early Irishmen managed to construct the "dolmens". If a capstone were surrounded by a group of the strongest men in the world, they would be unable to budge it at all—far less raise it off the ground. It is clear, therefore, that they must have been erected by some kind of mechanical means.

This knowledge of applied engineering is evidence that these people were intelligent and skilful. In addition, modern scholars have discovered that these tombs or circular shrines

A typical dolmen or prehistoric burial tomb. The large horizontal stone is called a capstone

were precision instruments of astronomy which would act as calendars to the days of the year.

Metal-working techniques may have been brought to Ireland and Britain by another immigrant group—the traders and smiths known as the Beaker people, named after the distinctive pots they made.

9

Gold sun discs found in some tombs dating back to this time suggest that sun-worship was practised.

The spectacular art of this pre-Christian era includes gold ornaments such as necklaces, brooches, belts and ear-rings. Many of these are made of paper-thin gold and are very delicately worked in geometric patterns of triangles and diamond shapes. (There is a fine collection of them in the National Museum in Dublin.) During this period, Irish gold and copper goods were traded as far as Central Europe; and tin was alloyed with copper to make bronze tools.

The next people to arrive in Ireland were the Celts who created the great Iron Age cultures which continued un-interrupted in Ireland and Scotland, because the Roman invaders, and later the Saxon invaders, never reached these countries. There were two waves of Celtic immigration. The first Celts came in about 500 B.C. from the Rhineland. They introduced improved agricultural implements, including the iron ploughshare and the two-ox plough. The main wave of Celtic immigration took place in about 300 B.C. This time, the people came from northern France and Brittany. They settled as miners, traders, horse-breeders and cattle-farmers. Weaving-combs and spindles were a standard part of their household equipment. Their smiths forged iron and bronze into swords, shields and horse-armour and they probably introduced chariot warfare into Britain and Ireland.

They built hill forts which were defended by men armed with slings and these, together with other remains, have provided us with much fascinating information about their way of life.

Though the Romans conquered most of Europe and came as far north as Britain, they never attempted to invade Ireland.

A two-headed stone figure from County Fermanagh, dating back to pre-Christian times

The Irish were, however, known to the Romans as fierce warriors who plundered the western provinces of the Roman Empire: Britain and Gaul (France). They raided these places frequently and carried off many captives to use as slaves in Ireland.

Early in the fifth century one of these raiding parties returned to Ireland with some prisoners. Among them was a youth who was put to work tending sheep on a mountainside in the north of Ireland. Eventually, this boy escaped from Ireland but he returned in A.D. 432—as a bishop. His name was Patrick. By the time he died, at the end of the century, he had travelled throughout the island and converted most of the people to Christianity.

St. Patrick is the patron saint of Ireland and St. Patrick's Day, March 17th, is celebrated by Irish people throughout the world. Every Irishman wears shamrock on that day, because legend has it that St. Patrick used the shamrock to illustrate his teaching of the Trinity.

For three centuries after the death of St. Patrick, art and religious learning flourished in Ireland. Monasteries and churches were built and Ireland earned for itself the name "Island of Saints and Scholars". Many wonderful examples of the art of this period can be seen today. The most famous is the Book of Kells which is in the library of Trinity College, Dublin. This is a copy of the four Gospels in Latin, illuminated with beautiful designs. It was written on vellum (fine parchment) by monks in the eighth century.

Saul, in County Down, where St. Patrick first preached. A tiny ancient chapel now stands on the site of his first church

Irish monks went out to Britain and to the continent of Europe and established monasteries there. They brought faith and learning to the pagan people who had overrun the Roman Empire. The Swiss canton (province) of St. Gall, for example, is named after the Irishman who built a monastery there. Another Irishman, St. Columba, is probably the best known of these monks, because of his work in Britain. He

13

A page from the Book
of Kells, showing a
portrait of Christ

established his monastery on Iona, one of the islands of the
Inner Hebrides.

This then was Ireland between the fifth and ninth centuries:
a land of peace, learning, faith and art.

The country was ruled by an *Ard-Ri*, or High-King, who
had his seat at Tara, Co. Meath. There were other kings who
ruled the provinces but they were all subject to the High-King.
These provinces still exist today; they are Ulster, Connaught,
Munster and Leinster.

This peaceful period ended late in the eighth century. Then

14

the Vikings came down from Scandinavia and began a series of raids along the east coast. The country could offer no defence against these warriors. They raided the monasteries and made off with books and treasures. They were so strong that they were able to establish a settlement at the mouth of the River Liffey—where the city of Dublin stands today.

It was not until the beginning of the eleventh century that a High-King who was strong enough to defeat the Danes came to power. He was King Brian Boru and he defeated the Danes at the Battle of Clontarf in 1014. Unfortunately, King Brian was himself killed in the battle. His death was followed by an unsettled period in Ireland while the other leaders struggled for power.

This left the country in a weak position to deal with the next horde of invaders, the Normans.

Having first established themselves in Britain, the Normans invaded Ireland in 1169 led by Strongbow (Richard de Clare, Earl of Pembroke). This was the beginning of centuries of strife in Ireland between the Irish and the Norman (later English) invaders.

The Normans adopted the language and customs of Ireland. Later, English kings were opposed by both the Irish and the Norman–Irish in their efforts to subdue the country. A decisive battle was fought at Kinsale in 1602. The English defeated the Irish and firmly established their power in Ireland. The Irish chiefs fled the country, their properties were confiscated and a series of plantations started. This was a scheme in which land was taken from the Irish and given to English settlers, usually as a reward for services to the Crown. The system was continued by Queen Elizabeth I and by James I and Oliver Cromwell.

It was these plantations which sowed the seeds of the fearful land troubles which beset Ireland in the nineteenth century.

In the sixteenth and seventeenth centuries, the efforts of English monarchs to introduce the reformed (Protestant) religion to Ireland met with little success. The people remained faithful to the Roman Catholic Church. For this they had to pay severe penalties.

Laws, known as the Penal Laws, were passed which took away civil and religious rights from Catholics. They were not allowed to vote or hold public office nor were they eligible for election to parliament. Catholic schools and teachers were banned and Catholic children were educated in so-called

Crom Castle, built in 1611 under the plantation scheme

"hedge schools". These illegal schools were held in the open air in fields; the school teachers travelled from place to place, teaching as they went.

Catholic churches and priests were banned. Priests often celebrated Mass in some lonely spot on a hillside while guards watched for the military patrols. In some places in Ireland the "Mass stones" which the priests used as altars can still be seen. Another sign of those unhappy times can be seen in Dublin. Though the population there is overwhelmingly Catholic, there are no Catholic churches in prominent sites in the centre of the city. To find them you have to go into the side streets, where they were built when permission was finally given.

In the eighteenth century, the rural areas of Ireland were sinking into misery and despair. The peasants lived in a state of poverty and oppression, but the city of Dublin flourished. While effective power remained in the hands of the English, a parliament was set up in Dublin in 1782 by the Protestant minority. It was during this period of prosperity that Dublin's noble buildings and graceful squares were built. These can still be seen today, as Dublin is one of the best preserved eighteenth-century cities in Europe.

However, the poor Irish Catholic peasant did not share in this prosperity. In 1798, the people rebelled against the authorities. The French sent troops to help this rebellion. But because they were badly armed and badly led, the people were soon crushed. There followed, in 1800, the Act of Union which abolished the Irish parliament and formally brought

Eighteenth-century doorways in Dublin, a city famous for its beautiful Georgian architecture

Ireland into the United Kingdom. The old Irish House of Parliament is still in existence and is now the Dublin head-quarters of the Bank of Ireland.

As a result of the Act of Union, the Irish were now represented at the House of Commons in Westminster. Daniel O'Connell, who defied the Penal Laws, became the first

18

Catholic elected to parliament. Through his efforts the Catholic Emancipation Act was passed in 1829, removing the more severe restrictions on Catholics. The people of Dublin named the city's principal thoroughfare after him—O'Connell Street.

During the nineteenth century the life of the Irish peasant became even worse. He was scratching out a living from a small patch of land, paying a high rent to an "absentee" landlord—that is, one living in England and not on his estate in Ireland. On their small plots of land, the Irish peasants each grew some grain and potatoes, and raised a cow or a pig or two. They sold the animals to pay their rent, and their staple food was the potato.

O'Connell Bridge which spans the River Liffey in Dublin, named after Daniel O'Connell

In 1845 a disease attacked the potato crop in Ireland and it could not be eaten. The Great Famine followed. At this time the population of Ireland was over eight million. By 1850, through starvation and emigration, it had fallen to about six million. Over the next fifty years, emigration drained away the population until, in 1900, it stood at about four million.

The Irish people went to Britain, the United States, Canada and Australia in their hundreds of thousands. In the great seaports of the world—in Liverpool, Boston and New York—huge Irish colonies grew. These people left their wretched homes in Ireland; weak and sometimes diseased, they travelled overseas under the most appalling conditions. It is quite a miracle that any survived. However, they did more than survive. They soon improved their lot and some of them helped to build up the prosperity of great nations.

One man who left Co. Cork at about this time was named William Ford. He became a farmer in the United States and prospered. He married and had a son. This son was Henry Ford, the great pioneer of the motor-car industry. Another man who left his small home near New Ross, Co. Wexford, was destined to have an equally famous descendant—John F. Kennedy, who became President of the United States.

The potato crop failed again for two or three years. The plight of the Irish peasant was desperate, between his hunger and his land troubles. Then a leader emerged named Michael Davitt. He founded the Land League. The object of the League was to get fair rents and other benefits for the Irish. As part of the campaign, the Irish would have nothing to do with any landlord who was not being fair to his tenants. One such landlord had an agent called Captain Boycott. He was treated in this way and thus gave rise to a new word in the English language—"boycott".

As a result of the agitation of the Land League and the efforts of Parnell (the leader of the Irish Party in the House of Commons at Westminster), a series of Land Acts were passed. By the beginning of the twentieth century, the aim of "land for the people" had to a great extent been achieved.

In the late nineteenth and early twentieth centuries the Irish Party had another object—Home Rule. They wanted self-government for Ireland. They were eventually successful in this too; but, just when an Act of Parliament giving at least some freedom had been passed, the First World War broke out, in 1914, and the new law was suspended.

However, not all of the people of Ireland favoured Home Rule. A strong body of opinion in the north-eastern part of Ulster (in the north of Ireland) favoured continued union with Britain. In 1912, Sir Edward Carson set up a provisional government there and formed an armed body pledged to oppose Home Rule by force.

The independence party struggling for Home Rule was called *Sinn Fein*. This is an Irish phrase and means "ourselves alone". They encouraged a great revival of national spirit and the many related organizations, such as the Irish Volunteers and the Trade Union Citizen Army, all had the same object—independence of Britain. Finally, in 1916, about a thousand men rose up against the British. They seized the principal buildings in Dublin and held them for a week. The headquarters of the Irish was the General Post Office in O'Connell Street and from there their leader, Patrick Pearse, proclaimed an independent Irish Republic.

At the end of the week's fighting the Irish surrendered. Hundreds of them were deported or gaoled. The fifteen leaders were executed by the British. This aroused the feelings of the people and, at the next General Election, in 1918, 78 of the 105 Irish seats at Westminster were won by the Sinn Fein Party.

The new members decided to boycott the parliament at Westminster. They set up their own assembly in Dublin, in January 1919, and constituted themselves as the National Parliament, or *Dail*, of Ireland. The British tried to suppress the Dail and its military wing, now called the Irish Republican Army. This led to extensive guerilla warfare throughout the country.

Finally, in 1921, a treaty was signed with Britain creating the Irish Free State, consisting of twenty-six counties. The remaining six counties in the north-eastern part of the country constituted Northern Ireland, which although largely self-governing, remained part of the United Kingdom.

Further tragedies were to befall Ireland before peace finally came. A civil war broke out between the supporters of the treaty and those who opposed it. The pro-treaty party favoured the establishment of the Free State within the Commonwealth, while their opponents supported the idea of a completely independent republic.

The Irish Free State government survived and, by 1923, the conflict was over. The governments of Northern Ireland and the Free State then got down to the task of creating the modern Ireland.

In 1937 the Irish Free State adopted a new constitution. The description "Free State" was abolished and the country became known as *Eire* which is the Irish name for Ireland.

In 1949, Eire withdrew from the British Commonwealth and became a sovereign independent republic, while Northern Ireland remained a part of the United Kingdom.

The People of Ireland

Like many of the other peoples of Europe, the Irish race is a mixture of native and invader. To the original Celts, who came to Ireland from mid-Europe, were added the Scandinavian invaders in the eighth century and the Normans in the twelfth century. In addition, the plantations of Ulster brought a large number of Scots to the north of Ireland. These newcomers settled down and inter-married with the native population.

Although there is no such thing as a typical Irishman, the Irish are generally lively, friendly and hospitable; and they are always ready to talk to a stranger. In fact, the Irishman is a born talker. The Irish have a considerable reputation for using words effectively, whether in writing or speech. They have always excelled in professions which require a good deal of talking—such as politics and law.

"Blarney" is a description you may have heard of an Irishman's talk. It was Queen Elizabeth I who first used the phrase "Blarney talk". The then Lord of Blarney, Cormac MacDermod MacCarthy, was engaged in a dispute with the Queen. She dismissed his eloquent pleas describing them as "Blarney". The legend then grew that whoever kissed the Blarney Stone in the castle at Blarney, Co. Cork, would receive the gift of eloquence.

Two languages are spoken in Ireland: Irish and English. Nowadays, the majority of the people speak English; but, up to the middle of the last century, Irish (or Gaelic, as it is sometimes called) was the language of the people. Today Irish is spoken as a native language only in certain areas along the western seaboard.

The Irish language is very similar to the Gaelic spoken in Scotland. Some Irish words have even found their way into the English language. "Galore" is the Irish *go leor*, i.e. to sufficiency. "Whiskey" (which the Irish invented) is *uisge beatha*, the water of life.

In the Irish Republic, Irish is the official language of the country, as laid down in the constitution of 1937. It is taught in all the schools of the country; indeed, in a large number of schools children are educated completely in Irish. They study Latin, mathematics, chemistry and physics all in Irish. Most of the people of Ireland have a knowledge of Irish but they seldom get an opportunity to use it, although there is a certain amount of Irish used in the newspapers and on radio and television.

Throughout the Irish Republic all signposts and street nameplates give their information in both Irish and English. In most cases the English name is the anglicized form of the old Irish name. Probably the most common prefix to appear is *Bally* which is the Irish word *baile*—"town". *Kil* is also common, as in Kilkenny. *Cill* is the Irish word for church; Kilkenny means the church of Canice. The use of *Kil* in a place name usually means that someone built a church there many years ago.

The contribution the Irish have made to English literature is astonishing, bearing in mind the size and population of the country. The great Irish writers, playwrights and poets include Oscar Wilde, Bernard Shaw and W. B. Yeats; Jonathan Swift, who wrote *Gulliver's Travels*, Oliver Goldsmith, Sean O'Casey and James Joyce.

The Irish are a very musical people, too, and they are fond of singing and dancing. There is an Irish song for every occasion—love songs and laments, lullabies and drinking songs, religious songs and humorous ones. Because of Ireland's unhappy history it is natural that many of her songs should be sad—songs of famine times and exile—but Irish dances are gay and lively. In the farmhouses in the Irish countryside, you can take part in a *ceili*—a succession of reels and jigs

26

danced to the accompaniment of a traditional Irish fiddler, mixed with songs and story-telling.

The musical instrument traditionally associated with Ireland is the harp, which is the national emblem of the country. Centuries ago bards (or wandering minstrels) travelled through Ireland singing songs to the accompaniment of their harps. These harps were not the large instruments we see on the concert platform today. They were much smaller and were

Irish dancing

easily carried. One of these old harps is preserved in the library of Trinity College, Dublin.

The bards sang for kings and chieftains and lived by their hospitality. If this hospitality was good the bards composed verses praising their hosts which they sang round the county. If it did not come up to their expectations the verses were not

This harp resembles the ones played by the Irish minstrels centuries ago. Now it provides music at the medieval banquets staged for visitors to the Bunratty Castle in County Clare

very complimentary to the hosts. It was a very pleasant life for the bards in the early days and naturally many young men wanted to join their ranks. Eventually, they became so numerous that the situation got out of hand and their numbers had to be reduced greatly.

The harp gradually disappeared from the Irish scene. The last of the great harp-players, O'Carolan, who was blind from youth, died in 1738. However, a large number of Irish girls still learn to play the harp at school, so it is possible today to hear the beautiful songs of Ireland sung and played as in the centuries gone by.

After the death of O'Carolan the fiddle and the pipes took the place of the harp as the principal instruments in Irish music. Irish pipes are called "Uilleann" pipes and they are not as shrill as the Scottish bagpipes. Their tone is more like that of the oboe.

The music of Ireland has not only survived the coming of radio and television but is now reaching a much wider audience in the cities and towns through these media.

There is one traditional Irish activity, however, which has not survived the coming of the modern means of communication—story-telling. The story-teller, or *seanachai* in Irish, had a huge supply of stories, some of them lasting an hour or more. He could hold his audience's interest with long tales of romance, adventure, or the ancient heroes of Ireland. Nowadays, it is only in the remoter parts of Ireland that you will come across a *seanachai*. But the tradition lives on. In Ireland

Irish musicians

today the telling of a tale is just as important as the subject-matter, and a variety of colourful phrases is included in every Irishman's story.

The Irish are frequently accused of living in the past. Perhaps this is because Irish history is rich with heroes, saints, scholars, kings, warriors, bards and poets. Every Irish child

30

learns the stories and legends of ancient Ireland at an early age. This knowledge of past glories helped to sustain nationalism in Ireland when Britain ruled the country.

A characteristic of the Celt is a belief in the existence of fairies, and this belief has always been strong in Ireland. The Irish word for fairy is *sidh* (pronounced *shee*) and this word is incorporated into place-names all over the country. The fairies of Ireland are considered to be a merry people. They live in mounds or small hills, usually with a ring of trees round the top, called a *rath*, or fairy fort. Probably the best known Irish fairy is the leprechaun. He is the shoemaker to the fairies and is reputed to have a crock of gold. If you can catch him and hold him with a fixed gaze he will part with his gold. However the leprechaun always manages to distract his captor and escape.

Equally famous is the banshee (*bean-sidhe*, or fairy woman). The banshee foretells a death in some families by wailing round the house at night.

Stories about these little people are told in Ireland along with tales of the legendary and the more recent heroes. The result is that the myths merge with the facts and though the modern Irishman will tell you that he does not believe in fairies, he may add that he hopes he will never meet one.

As you would expect in an agricultural country, Irish food is very good. The Irish eat plenty of meat—beef, mutton, pork and ham. Potatoes and cabbage are the two most popular vegetables to accompany the meat. In spite of the fact that they live on an island, the Irish do not eat a great deal of fish. Home-made bread is very common and very tasty. There are two kinds, both made in flat round loaves—one white, called soda bread, and the other a brown wheaten loaf.

The Irish are great tea-drinkers too. Their consumption per head is one of the highest in the world. In every Irish farmhouse the kettle is kept on the boil ready to provide a cup of tea for the visitor. When it comes to stronger beverages the Irish drink whiskey, usually with a little water, and stout— the black beer brewed in Dublin and Cork.

The people of Ireland have a great capacity for enjoying life but they are also a deeply religious people. Religion has always played an important part in the lives of Irishmen.

St. Patrick's grave in Downpatrick, near Saul in County Down

From A.D. 432, when St. Patrick brought Christianity to Ireland, the country has remained staunchly Christian. Of the 4,250,000 people in Ireland today, 3,250,000 are Roman Catholics. The remainder are principally Church of Ireland (Anglican) and Presbyterian.

Sport is a great passion of the Irish. Football of every kind is played in Ireland, as well as golf and tennis. As is to be expected in an island with two thousand miles of coast line, swimming and sailing are very popular.

The Irish horse is world-famous; hacking, pony-trekking, hunting, show-jumping, flat-racing and steeplechasing all have many followers. (Steeplechasing originated in County Cork in 1752. The horses raced from Buttevant to Doneraile church steeple, hence the name for the present-day sport.)

The most popular games in Ireland are hurling and Gaelic football. The football has points of similarity with both rugby and soccer. Hurling is a fast, exciting game played with a long wooden curved stick and a ball about the size of a tennis ball. The All-Ireland Football and Hurling finals attract eighty thousand spectators each to Croke Park in Dublin every September.

About half the population of Ireland lives on the land. Before the modern growth of the cities of Dublin and Belfast, the rural population was much higher. Many of the present-day city- and town-dwellers are the sons and daughters of

A view of the Boyne Valley in County Meath. Hunting is a popular sport in this county

farmers. These close ties with the slower pace of rural life probably account for the Irishman's relaxed attitude to the world—relaxed, that is, in relation to someone born and bred to the complex life of a large industrial city. But Ireland is far from being a backward country. The development of the economy has been considerable in recent years. In spite of the changes taking place, the Irish are managing to retain a balanced view of life.

Cities and Towns

Ireland has no natural resources such as coal, oil or iron ore. So the economy of the island is largely based on agriculture. Not unnaturally, therefore, there are few large industrial cities in Ireland.

Dublin, on the River Liffey, is the capital of the Irish Republic and has a population of 600,000. Belfast, the capital of Northern Ireland, has 450,000 people. The next largest cities are Cork and Limerick in the south and Derry in the north.

The earliest recorded reference to Dublin dates from A.D. 140. The name is the Irish *Dubh Linn*, meaning "dark pool". The Danes established a fort there in the ninth century and the Normans captured Dublin soon after they landed in Ireland in the twelfth century. In 1171, King Henry II, the Norman King of England, gave Dublin its first charter, by which it was granted the rights and privileges enjoyed by other cities of the realm.

The eighteenth century was Dublin's most colourful period. During this time many great public buildings, fine squares and wide streets were added to the city. Unfortunately, much of the centre of Dublin was destroyed during the fighting for independence between 1916 and 1921.

Today the city is a busy modern capital, the seat of the government of the Irish Republic. Its situation, on Dublin Bay, where the Liffey flows into the sea, makes it one of the most attractive cities in Europe. There are mountains a few miles south of the city and beaches within a fifteen-minute drive from O'Connell Street. At the week-ends and during the long summer evenings, Dubliners trek out of the city in their thousands to enjoy the sea or mountain air. The sea breezes keep Dublin free of the smoke and dirt normally associated with large cities.

Dublin is a busy seaport which handles a large part of Ireland's trade. The industry of Dublin is mixed; probably the city's most famous product is Guinness—a dark beer first brewed by Arthur Guinness by the side of the Liffey in 1759. The brewery he founded there is visited by thousands of people every year.

The Normans founded the two great cathedrals of Dublin in the twelfth century. They are St. Patrick's, of which Jonathan Swift was once Dean, and Christ Church. One of the most interesting churches in Dublin is the seventeenth-century St. Michan's. It attracts thousands of visitors annually, not to admire the architecture but to visit the vaults. These vaults have a peculiar dry atmosphere and, as a result, bodies which have lain there for centuries have remained perfectly preserved. Their skin is dark brown but is otherwise quite soft and lifelike.

Dublin Castle, in the centre of the city, was built in the

Trinity College, Dublin

thirteenth century and was formerly the residence of the British Viceroys and the headquarters of the British in Ireland. It is now used by the government of the Republic for various purposes and it houses the State Papers and Genealogical Office. The inauguration of the President of the Irish Republic takes place in the State Apartments of the Castle, after the presidential elections which are held every seven years.

Near Dublin Castle stands Trinity College. This university was founded by Queen Elizabeth I in 1591. Although in the heart of the city, it is a very beautiful and picturesque place with fine buildings, cobbled quadrangles, green playing-fields and tree-lined walks. The Library has the privilege of receiving a copy of every book printed in Great Britain or Ireland. It has over half a million books and manuscripts, the most famous being the Book of Kells.

Opposite Trinity College is the Bank of Ireland. This fine building was the Irish House of Parliament until 1800. It is only one of the many splendid examples of eighteenth-century architecture which can be seen around the city.

Dublin is quite a gay city and the people take full advantage of the many opportunities for amusement which the city provides. Dubliners like the social life and the many bars and cafés are filled with people talking—and singing too, as a number of bars feature traditional Irish music. Drama flourishes in Dublin, too, and the city supports four major theatres. The best known is the Abbey Theatre where many world-famous actors and actresses have begun their careers.

Dubliners are very fortunate to have on their doorstep a vast public park, the Phoenix Park. Apart from the zoo, it consists mainly of open spaces with playing-fields for football, cricket and polo; but it also houses the official residence of the President of the Republic.

About 160 kilometres (100 miles) north of Dublin is the great industrial city of Belfast. It is the capital of Northern Ireland. Belfast is a fairly modern city which developed very quickly with industrialization in the nineteenth century. It is a city of many industries but the two for which it is renowned are linen and shipbuilding. Shipyards were first founded on the River Lagan in 1791. Since that date, Belfast has built some of the largest ships in the world. The *Titanic*, which struck an

A view of the Belfast shipyards. In the foreground is the *Canberra*, under construction

iceberg on her maiden voyage trip to New York in 1912 and was lost with 1,500 people aboard, was built at Belfast. She was the largest ship in the world at that time. In more recent times, the *Canberra* was also built at the great shipyards of Belfast.

Belfast is a bustling, thriving city. The port, which is the largest in Ireland, deals with a huge volume of trade. The people have a reputation for being hard-headed businessmen but they also share the Irishman's love of good talk and music.

In the centre of Belfast is Donegall Square. This is dominated by the vast City Hall, built in 1906. From here the busy shopping streets of Belfast fan out. Because it is a relatively modern city it has few buildings of historic interest. However, just

Belfast City Hall in Donegall Square

Stormont, the parliament buildings just outside Belfast. They were built in 1928 of Portland stone on a plinth of grey Irish granite quarried in the Mountains of Mourne

outside Belfast, on a magnificent site on high ground, stand the Northern Ireland parliament buildings. They were built in 1928.

To the north of the city is Cave Hill, rising to over three hundred metres (about one thousand feet). It is a great natural park and, being very near the city centre, is a very popular place for the people of Belfast.

South of Belfast in the county of Down are the Mountains of Mourne, one of the many beautiful places in Ireland about which songs have been written. Near by is the town of Downpatrick, where St. Patrick is reputed to have been buried.

41

One of the world's outstanding geological curiosities is in County Antrim—the Giant's Causeway. The Irish name for the phenomenon is, typically, a romantic one—the giant's stepping-stones—but the truth is more ordinary. Cooling lava split the rock into many regular columns, mostly with six sides each, to create this wonderful spectacle.

Also in the province of Ulster is Lough Neagh—the largest lake in Ireland or Great Britain.

North-west of Belfast is the historic city of Derry. St. Columba founded a monastery here in A.D. 546 and later a town grew around it. In the seventeenth century the city and surrounding area was granted to the citizens of London by King James II. The city became known as Londonderry. (The beautiful, traditional Irish melody known as the *Londonderry Air* was first written down at Limavady in the county of Londonderry.) Londonderry is a walled city and the old walls are wonderfully preserved. There are four old city gates still in existence.

Donegal, the most northerly county of Ireland, is famous for its tweed and for its lovely scenery. It also includes Lough Derg. On this lake is an island which for 1,500 years has been

The Giant's Causeway

a place of pilgrimage. Each year hundreds of people each spend three days on the island, barefooted, praying and fasting—they are allowed one "meal" a day of black tea and dry bread.

South of Donegal is the county of Sligo. The poet W. B. Yeats loved this part of the country and much of his work reflects this love. On Lough Gill is the tiny island which Yeats made famous in his poem *The Lake Isle of Innisfree*.

Among the best-known towns is Galway, in the Irish Republic. Galway is a pleasant market town, situated on the west coast of Ireland, on Galway Bay. It is a great favourite with Irish people as a holiday centre. It had a long tradition of trading with Spain for many centuries; traces of Spanish influence may still be seen around the town.

Part of County Galway is known as Connemara. This is a region of Ireland where Irish is spoken as the everyday language of the people and many of the old crafts and traditions are kept alive. It is also the original home of the famous ponies of that name.

The Bishop's Gate through the famous walls of Derry. In the background is the Guildhall. It is still possible to walk round the walls which are wonderfully preserved in spite of their great age

Galway Cathedral

Out in Galway Bay are the Aran Islands. The traditional Irish way of life is best preserved on these islands. The islanders speak Irish, make their own clothes and shoes, and fish in the traditional currachs—small boats made of a wooden frame with a tarred canvas cover.

South of Galway is the city of Limerick, on the River Shannon. Limerick is an industrial and market town with great historical connections. It has been the scene of many battles and sieges. The battle-scarred King John's Castle, which stands by the river near the city centre, was erected in the thirteenth century.

45

Currachs on Aran

Modern Limerick owes much of its prosperity to the development of Shannon Airport as a great international airport. This was developed soon after the Second World War as a vital link in transatlantic communications. With the development of long-range jet aircraft, however, the need for re-fuelling stops at Shannon no longer existed and the airport's future did not look very promising. But by clever expansion

46

of the region's tourist attractions and the creation of an industrial estate, the authorities assured the future of Shannon and made it once again a major link in transatlantic travel.

Cork is the principal city in the south of Ireland. It is a major seaport and manufacturing city. Like many other Irish towns and cities, it began as a monastic settlement in the sixth century. It is very beautifully situated in the valley of the River Lee.

A view of the River Shannon, not far from Shannon Airport

A view of Cobh, which is situated in Cork Harbour, not far from the city of Cork. The port is dominated by St. Colman's Cathedral which stands on the hill overlooking the waterfront

In the county of Cork is the famous Blarney Castle and to the east of the county is Youghal, a small town of which Sir Walter Raleigh was once mayor. The house he lived in is still intact and tradition has it that it was here that he smoked the first tobacco and grew the first potatoes in Europe.

Cobh, about twenty-four kilometres (fifteen miles) out of Cork, is the port of call for the great transatlantic shipping lines.

The Castles of Ireland

How many castles would you expect to find in Ireland? Fifty, eighty or a hundred? County Limerick alone boasts 400, County Cork over 300 and the counties of Galway and Tipperary over 250 each. There are over 3,000 castles in Ireland and not one is without its own history of romance, high living, treachery, battles, boiling tar, captives' heads on spikes and, of course, the inevitable ghosts.

The first castles were built by the Normans in order to maintain their authority. Some of their earliest forts were not made of stone but were just high mounds topped by wooden towers and surrounded by stout palisades. This kind of structure is known as a "motte-and-bailey" and ruins of them still can be seen. The motte is the high and steep mound. The bailey is a raised platform beside it. Around each of them was a strong barrier of tree trunks. A gate led into the bailey

The Rock of Cashel in Tipperary. The remains at Cashel include the old Archbishop's Castle dating from the fifteenth century. The Irish countryside boasts many beautiful castles, some of them still in very good repair

and a wooden gangway ran from the bailey to the top of the motte.

When these castles were attacked the families who lived in them were sent into the bailey along with the animals and valuables, and a strong guard of bowmen on the motte discouraged attackers. Good examples of these forts still exist at Knockgraffon, Kilfeacle and in the college grounds of Newbridge in County Kildare, as well as at Breenmount and Cloncurry in County Louth and through areas of Leinster, Munster and Ulster.

The great castles began to be built soon after the Norman invasion. As "Lord of Ireland" the king required stout stone fortresses to protect those who ruled for him against turbulent Irish princes and, indeed, against Norman barons who took advantage of the distance between them and the supreme authority resident in England.

King John, who was later forced to sign the Magna Carta, was sent to Ireland while his brother Richard the Lionheart was on the English throne. During his stay in Ireland, John is reputed to have been responsible for the building of many great castles including Dublin, Carlingford, Limerick and Trim. The latter, with its great central keep and its long wall, interspersed at intervals with huge towers, encloses over three acres. At one period in his life, Henry, the Prince of Wales who later became King Henry V of England, was imprisoned in one of these huge towers. Centuries later, the Duke of Wellington (who later defeated Napoleon) played there as a boy.

We are inclined to associate castles with hideous battles and dark dungeons, but there were times when torches shone on silk and jewels and minstrels played from their gallery to entertain the diners in the hall below.

Now, in the twentieth century, such activities still continue. In Bunratty Castle banquets are still served in full medieval splendour and pageantry all the year round. As the traveller enters the castle he is handed a goblet of mead, an alcoholic beverage made from honey and based on an ancient recipe.

Before dinner he is allowed to wander around and study the priceless tapestries and furnishings dating back to the fifteenth and sixteenth centuries. After dinner is announced the guests enter the great hall. There they find a high table and other great oak refectory tables leading off it at right angles. Dinner includes oak-smoked salmon, and guinea-fowl baked in cream and cider sauce and served on a bed of wild rice. The meal is eaten with a dagger; it is washed down with claret. During the festivities guests are entertained by a harpist and by singers dressed in period costume singing traditional airs.

The present Bunratty Castle was built by the MacNamara family in 1450, but its history goes back to the thirteenth century. It was once home of the O'Briens, Earls of Thomond and Limerick, descendants of King Brian Boru who freed Ireland from the invading Danes in 1014. The original gardens were most impressive, being composed mainly of mosaic-patterned cobblestones. These gardens are now being excavated and should prove of great interest.

On a rugged promontory in County Galway is Dunguaire Castle. This is a small Norman fortress but it has been put to a new use in the twentieth century. Visitors to the castle can now hear readings from the works of such famous Irish writers as Sean O'Casey, George Bernard Shaw and the poet W. B. Yeats.

Knappogue Castle, Co. Clare, was also built by the Mac-Namara family in 1467. Its architecture is more varied than that of Bunratty and it was occupied as an ordinary home until

1923. Here, too, the visitor can enjoy the full splendour of a sumptuous medieval banquet.

A number of the castles in Ireland have been restored and made functional. Kilkenny Castle, Co. Kilkenny, for example, is noted for its progressive Design Centre which is housed in the beautiful stable block.

Ashford Castle at Cong, built for the Guinness family in the nineteenth century is now a luxury hotel with lovely grounds for walking in and a lake for boating.

Another link with the O'Brien clan is Dromoland Castle near Shannon Airport. This castle, which was built in 1570, now combines the original charm of the old building with all the comforts and amenities of a luxurious resort—into

Kilkenny Castle, now used to house a modern design centre

which it has been converted. The vast grounds include an 18-hole golf-course and facilities for riding, shooting and boating.

The latest castle to be converted back to a place of residence for the traveller is Kilkea Castle which was built by the Anglo-Norman knight Walter de Riddleford in 1180. It now becomes the oldest inhabited castle in Ireland, having over fifty bedrooms and 44·5 hectares (110 acres) of beautifully laid out grounds.

Of all the Irish castles perhaps Blarney is the best known. All that now remains of it is the massive square keep, 25·2 metres (83 feet) high. Below the battlements is set the famous Blarney Stone which is said to bestow its gift of oratory on anyone who kisses it.

The Emerald Isle

Ireland is an island of nearly 82,880 square kilometres (32,000 square miles). Its greatest length is 486 kilometres (302 miles); its greatest width 304 kilometres (189 miles). The traveller is never more than 160 kilometres (100 miles) from the sea. In addition, because of the 800 lakes and rivers of inner Ireland, it is possible to travel from Dublin in the east to Sligo in the north-west without ever losing sight of water for more than half an hour.

The first impression the visitor receives is that of rich greenness, hence the nickname "Emerald Isle". The pasture-land is a rich green because there is a considerable amount

Lough Na Crannog, County Antrim, one of Ireland's 800 lakes

The Middle Lake, Killarney. Here the climate is so temperate that palms grow

of rain and because the winters are mild and the summers temperate. The sunniest months are May and June; snow is very rare in the winter except in the mountains.

Ireland's geographical position is interesting; if you were to take a boat and sail due south from Ireland you would not hit another land mass until you came to the South Pole. To the west you have to sail over 3,800 kilometres (2,400 miles) across the Atlantic Ocean before you reach the continent of North America. (History records that Columbus did just that—Galway, on the west coast of Ireland was his last port of call before he set out for the "New World".)

Ireland is the most westerly part of Europe. Her nearest neighbour is Britain which, on the map, looks like her dancing partner. She is separated by the width of between approximately 100 and 200 kilometres (60 and 120 miles) of the Irish Channel, except in the north-east where she leans into Scotland and is only separated from that country by thirty-two kilometres (twenty miles) of sea.

Ireland is divided into four provinces and thirty-two counties. The four provinces are Ulster (nine counties) in the north; Munster (six counties) in the south; Leinster (twelve

A view of the Antrim coast road which runs parallel with the Irish Channel coast for ninety-six kilometres (sixty miles) from Larne to Portrush

counties) in the east; and Connacht (five counties) in the west.

Viewed from above (in an aeroplane), Ireland looks like a basin, since she has a central plain ringed by a coastal belt of highlands. Much of the plain is rich agricultural land; farming is the country's principal industry and farm produce the major export.

The geographical position and shape of Ireland provides many natural advantages and has an interesting effect on the outlook of her people. Geographically remote, her people's way of life is not wholly dominated by the power of modern industry and the speed of twentieth-century civilization. There is an old saying: "When God made time, He made plenty of it", and in Ireland this is true. Life for the Irish is not a gallop, but something to be enjoyed at a walk or leisurely trot.

The motorist, walker and climber find the roads are among the most unpopulated in Europe and there are no traffic queues. More often than not the motorist finds that when he does share the road, he does so with a herd of sheep or cows, or with some horse-drawn vehicle.

The scenery is not spoilt by industrial chimneys and belching smoke; nor disfigured by mountains of slag. The rivers do not run muddy from the waste of mills; and the salmon come up from the sea through bright clear water.

The Shannon is the largest river in the United Kingdom and Ireland. It is over 370 kilometres (230 miles) long and drains one-fifth of Ireland. Along its course, the Shannon

Donkeys are still found in Irish country areas as a means of transport or as beasts of burden. This photograph was taken in Connemara

broadens out into a number of lakes (or loughs). An attractive feature of these is that they can boast many interesting little islands with fascinating names such as Holy Island, King Island, Friars Island, Nuns Island and Goose Island. Farmers swim their cattle across to graze on some of these islands. Others contain remnants of great archaeological interest because the Shannon provided natural and peaceful surroundings which appealed to the early Christian fathers.

Some of Ireland's most beautiful scenery: Lough Veagh, County Donegal

Monasteries sprang up, from the fifth century on, and endured until they were destroyed by the Viking invaders who arrived in their warships. The monks from these monasteries spread Christianity to Scotland and as far west as Germany during the fifth and sixth centuries.

Other great early Christian settlements are to be found on the small islands off the Irish coast, such as the Skelligs, just south of the magnificent ring of Kerry.

The ring of Kerry is a high mountain range stretching for over 160 kilometres (100 miles) around the Kerry Peninsula. On sunny days, the shadows of small white clouds float like seagulls across the mountain slopes. The highest of these mountains, Carrantuo-hill, is over 1,040 metres (3,414 feet) high. The popular ascent to the top is by Hag's Glen and the Devil's Ladder to the summit. Names like these originated in Gaelic and describe the atmosphere of the remoter parts where fact and fiction blend in legend.

Ireland is unique in that she exists in the midst of modern European development and yet still remains unspoilt.

Industry

Because of Ireland's relatively low population, the home market for manufactured goods is small. This means that the country relies heavily on overseas outlets for her products. This, and the fact that she has very few natural resources, has limited the range of profitable industries in Ireland, and has caused much of the country to remain agricultural.

Ireland's largest single industry is agriculture which accounts for as much as a quarter of her total export trade. She does, however, derive some economic benefit from such mineral deposits as have been found. For example, anthracite is mined in Kilkenny and Tipperary, coal in Leitrim, and gypsum (the raw material of plaster of Paris which is used in hospitals for mending broken limbs) comes from Cavan. This gypsum is also used in the production of plasterboard for the building trade. Barytes, an ingredient in white paint, comes from Cork and Sligo. Recently, valuable deposits of zinc, lead and copper were found in Galway and Meath. In addition, limestone and chalk are found throughout the country, with particular concentrations in Northern Ireland. These are used for the manufacture of cement and are important for farming.

While Ireland's industry relies on gas and electricity as power sources, the source of heat for domestic purposes comes mainly from peat, used for both heating and cooking—at least in country areas. Peat (or turf as it is called in Ireland) gives off a pleasant aroma as it burns and makes Irish homes cosy and warm in the winter.

The Irish textile industry provides employment for large numbers of the working population. Linen is the key product. Specialization in linen was originally based on the local production of flax (the raw material from which linen is manufactured) but this is no longer significant. It is from the north-east, and particularly from Belfast itself, that the famous Irish linen comes. It is made up into table cloths, luncheon mats, supper and glass cloths (hand-painted in gay floral or traditional Irish patterns), blouses and handkerchiefs.

Another major industry for which Ireland is famous is ship-building. The big shipyards in Belfast, where the *Titanic* and the *Canberra* were built, employ nearly 26,000 men.

In common with those of many other countries, Ireland's old established heavy industries are in decline. In both Northern Ireland and the Irish Republic steps have been

Down Plain, County Down. Agriculture produces one quarter of Ireland's exports

Peat stacked outside a typical Irish thatched cottage in Kerry

taken to encourage large companies from abroad to establish factories there. This has provided many jobs for young people who otherwise might have had to emigrate.

To attract new industry many benefits are offered to companies. For example, in the Irish Republic, until the year

2,000, the new industries will pay only ten per cent tax on profits. Cash grants (of up to sixty per cent) are given for the cost of machinery and equipment; and the full cost of training workers is covered.

There are now more than fifty American companies operating in Ireland as well as many British, German, Dutch and Japanese manufacturers.

Since the early 1970s the governments have worked to establish Ireland as a centre for new technology and have encouraged electronic manufacturers to set up there. As a result of this policy, there are over ninety such companies in Ireland. They employ some 15,000 people and by 1985 this figure is expected to have doubled.

The educational system has had to adapt itself quickly to this new development to make sure that there are enough students coming through to meet the needs of these new industries. Today, all universities and technical colleges offer courses in computer studies.

The transport of goods into, through and out of Ireland is efficient because communications are excellent and regular. There are daily sailings from Irish ports to Britain, and regular sailings to Europe and North America. Daily air services link Dublin, Shannon and Cork with all the main industrial and commercial centres in Britain, and also with Europe and North America. There is also an efficient internal railway system, and road transport is completely free of traffic congestion.

Irish factories now produce a wide variety of consumer goods including clothing, footwear, flour, sugar and a variety of other food products, wool and cotton goods, soap, pottery, glass, cutlery, cement, paper, tobacco, steel, electrical equipment, paint and furniture.

Side by side with these industries, the traditional industries for which Ireland is famous still thrive. Visitors when they come to Ireland like to return with an Aran sweater made of "bawneen", the rain-resistant, undyed wool. These Aran sweaters were originally made on the Aran Isles by the wives and mothers of fishermen. Each sweater carried the family pattern so that is a man were drowned at sea, which unfortunately was frequent, he could be recognized by his kin. Even more characteristically Irish are Aran "pampooties"— moccasins made from cowhide with the hair left on, and the Aran "crios", which is a belt made of numerous woven coloured strands. Sweaters are not Ireland's only contribution

Waterford glass

to high fashion in the world's shops. From the cottages of Donegal, in the north-west, comes tweed which is justly famous in fashion houses the world over.

The city of Waterford in the south-east is the home of decorative cut crystal glassware. Since the eighteenth century, the craftsmen of Waterford have created their wares in these furnace workshops. Their products range from sherry glasses to the chandeliers which are blown and shaped piece by piece while the glass is molten hot. The designs are based on traditional patterns now recognized throughout the world.

Among Ireland's luxury products are the objects of art and pieces of jewellery made from rich green marble which is quarried in Connemara. These are either exported or sold as attractive souvenirs to visitors. Dublin itself also manufactures jewellery, made from enamel. Often, the brooches and rings are based on the outstanding designs found in the ancient Book of Kells.

Farming and Fishing

One of the most noticeable things about the Irish countryside, apart from the fresh green colour, is the size of the fields which cover almost the entire country. Irish farms are small—some have as little as six hectares (under fifteen acres) of land—and each farm is divided into smaller fields separated by hedgerows or (in the west of the country) by stone walls. Although these small fields are pretty to look at, especially if you are flying over the land in an aeroplane, they do not help the Irish farmer to get the most he can from Ireland's greatest natural resource—her rich and fertile earth.

The Gulf Stream, a warm current of water which flows across the Atlantic from the Gulf of Mexico, washes the shores of Ireland and gives it a mild climate all the year round. The country has no extremes of heat or cold; it is not unusual for a winter to pass without severe frost or snow.

Because of these two factors—good land and a mild climate —agriculture has always been the most important single industry in Ireland.

Ownership of the land, as we have seen from the history of Ireland, has always played an important part in the lives of Irishmen. Today the vast majority of Irish farmers own their

Irish farmland, showing the typical low stone walls which divide off small plots

land and most of the farms are family farms, run by the fathers and their sons. The womenfolk, in addition to running the farm household, usually tend the poultry—chickens, hens and turkeys.

Farming in Ireland is usually mixed. The farmer will raise some cattle, or perhaps sheep, and at the same time grow a variety of crops. This explains the large number of small fields: each grows a different crop.

Towards the western seaboard the land is not as good as in other parts of the country. The soil is thin and the fields are stony. Here are to be found the smallest—and most picturesque—of the Irish farms, complete with the typical Irish farmhouse, with whitewashed walls and thatched roof.

Elsewhere the land is excellent. Cattle are bred in all parts of the country and are usually sent to graze in the great plains of the midlands. Here the even rainfall ensures a good growth of grass and the cattle are fattened prior to being exported, alive, to Britain.

There is a large cattle market near Phoenix Park in Dublin. Here over 10,000 cattle and sheep are sold every week to overseas buyers. In addition, over 100,000 tonnes of carcass meat are exported each year to Britain and Europe. The Irish farmer has

A whitewashed cottage with a thatched roof, a familiar sight in all country districts throughout Ireland

Sheep grazing in a mountain pass area in Donegal

prospered since the country joined the European Economic Community (E.E.C.). Britain was always the traditional market for Irish meat and dairy produce but membership of the E.E.C. has meant greatly expanded markets.

Sheep-farming is becoming more popular in Ireland. The mountain areas are ideal for sheep-grazing. A car-driver travelling through the remoter parts of Ireland will probably have sheep as his sole companions.

In the winter the cattle are fed on hay. During the summer the hay is cut and stacked in small cocks which are left to dry in the fields for a few weeks. Later, the hay is gathered in to a barn and built up into a large stack ready for winter use.

Not all the cattle in Ireland are slaughtered for beef, however. There is a flourishing dairy farming industry, especially in the province of Munster. The cows grazing on these rich pasture-lands produce high yields of milk from which butter and cheese are made. Some of these products are consumed on the home market but a large proportion goes to Britain and continental Europe.

The same rich grassland which produces the beef and dairy cattle also makes horse-breeding a very profitable business in Ireland. Each year millions of pounds' worth of Irish horses are exported to all parts of the world for breeding, racing, show-jumping and hunting. You have probably seen pictures of the Emperor Napoleon mounted on a white horse. This beautiful charger, Marengo, was bred in Co. Wexford, Ireland.

Alongside the fields where the cattle and horses graze, the Irish farmer grows a variety of grain and root crops. Wheat, potatoes, barley and sugar beet are grown extensively. Brewing beer and distilling whiskey are important Irish industries and a good deal of the barley grown is used for these purposes. The entire sugar beet crop is bought by the Irish Sugar Co., a State concern which operates four sugar-making factories in Ireland.

Each year, as industrialization grows and the mechanization of farm work increases, the number of people working on the land in Ireland falls. But the production of food will always be a vital factor in the Irish economy. In addition, the absence of other natural resources limits the process of industrialization. It seems, therefore, that Ireland will remain the "Emerald Isle" for the foreseeable future.

Large areas of Ireland are covered by peat bogs. Peat, or turf—as the Irish call it—is the traditional Irish fuel. For centuries it has been cut by hand with a *sleann*, which is like a V-shaped spade. The pieces of turf, brown in colour and very wet, are stacked in small piles to dry and harden in the sun. When dry they are taken home and stacked by the side of the farmer's house to be used as fuel during the winter. The smell of a turf fire is very pleasant and the smoke it gives off is light blue in colour. Unlike coal, it is very clean to handle. It burns itself out into a white ash.

In recent years a State body called Bord na Mona (The Peat Board) has developed the production of peat on a large scale. Huge cutting machines move across the bogs cutting vast amounts annually. This peat is used in industry and as a source of power. The government of the Irish Republic has built a number of peat-burning power-stations close to the bogs and these stations supply nearly half of the electricity used in the Republic. Bord na Mona also produces milled peat which is compressed and looks, and feels, like a dark brown brick. This is used by the Irish people in their homes and is also used to heat offices and factories.

Cutting turf or peat, the traditional fuel

Another product won from the Irish bogs is peat moss—peat in powder and flake form. This is used extensively by gardeners.

Unlike most coal-mining, which is done far underground, peat is taken from the surface of the bogs and it is very seldom necessary to dig below three metres (about ten feet) for it. There are many years of life left in Irish bogs and the industry will be a flourishing one for a long time to come.

Ireland has over 3,200 kilometres (2,000 miles) of coastline but its fishing industry is not as developed as might be expected. The principal varieties of fish in the seas around Ireland are herring, whiting, cod, haddock, lobsters and crayfish.

There was once a thriving fishing industry in Ireland; in the last century over 100,000 people were engaged in catching fish and salting them for export to the United States and elsewhere. But the upheaval which followed the Great Famine upset the fishing industry and it went into a decline.

Recently, however, efforts have been made to develop the industry. In the Irish Republic the Sea Fisheries Board, or Bord Iascaigh Mhara to give it its Irish title, has made it easier for the fishermen to buy new boats and equipment. New boat-yards have been opened around the country for the building of fishing-boats. The Board also has factories for processing fish and is always looking for new outlets for the produce of Ireland's rich coastal waters.

These waters attract deep-sea trawlers from all over Europe. The Russians, the Spaniards, the French and the Dutch all come to fish off the coast of Ireland. One of the most popular places is Dunmore East in Co. Waterford. When the herring shoals are off the coast, the town and harbour are full of fishermen and boats of all nationalities.

The Irish Republic has a small Naval Service whose principal activity is to prevent these foreign fishermen fishing

A view of the harbour at Ardglass, an important herring fishery centre in County Down

within the territorial waters of Ireland. In Northern Ireland these duties are undertaken by British fisheries protection vessels.

There is a good demand for Irish lobsters, crabs and crayfish in France and many fishermen find it profitable to run a small boat with some lobster-pots, and fish the waters close to the coast for this popular delicacy. They mark the pots which lie on the sea-bed with brightly coloured floating buoys. If you stand on a cliff-top you can see the fishermen moving along from buoy to buoy, pulling up each pot, taking out the catch, re-stocking the pot with bait and sinking it again. The catch is taken ashore and kept in large water tanks until it can be shipped to its destination.

Dublin Bay prawns are another well known seafood delicacy. These are caught in Dublin Bay by fishing fleets working out of the small harbours near the city of Dublin. You can actually eat Dublin Bay prawns in some seafood restaurants in Dublin a few hours after they have been landed.

Although the inland fisheries on the many lakes and rivers of Ireland are mainly used by tourists, there is a flourishing salmon-fishing industry. Enormous quantities of salmon are exported to Britain each year. Round Achill Island, off the west coast of Ireland, some commercial shark fishing is also done. The sharks are harmless basking sharks which visit the shores of Ireland during the summer.

Sports and Pastimes

Ireland is the land of the horse. Race-going is a national pastime. There are 150 fixtures throughout the season, including the Irish Derby which is run at Curragh, each June. The winner of the Irish Derby collects a large cash prize and this attracts entries from international racing stables the world over.

Of the thirty Irish race courses, several of the leading ones are within easy reach of Dublin. It is here that many of the popular events, such as the Irish Grand National, the St. Leger, the Guineas and the famous Punchestown Races are run.

Every year thousands of visitors gather to see the Dublin Horse Show where the finest show-jumpers, with their riders dressed in smart riding-habits (or uniform) and highly polished boots, compete for coveted prizes.

The keen horseman who lives in Ireland or visits the country is always welcome to participate in other riding activities too.

Pony trekking

There are no fewer than thirty packs of hounds, thirty-five of harriers and two staghound hunts. In addition, there is also plenty of pony-trekking and hacking. This, of course, goes on all the year round. A typical day's trekking begins by setting off at nine o'clock in the morning. For three hours the party climbs up into the purple mountains, occasionally cantering and galloping over deserted moorland, until a small two-roomed white cottage is reached. Here the farmer's wife gives the riders a simple meal and the horses are fed, watered and rested. In the afternoon the trek down to the lake far below begins. From this distance it looks inky black. At about five o'clock the lakeside is reached. But, by this time, the water has changed to a transparent blue. A trot round the lakeside leads to a country road, bordered on both sides by vivid yellow gorse. This, in turn, leads back to the stables which come into view as dusk descends.

Fishing is the second most popular pastime. There are lakes and rivers throughout Ireland which provide a fisherman's paradise. They are stocked with salmon, brown trout, pike,

Pike fishing on the River Finn in County Monaghan

Trout fishing

bream, rudd and tench—to name but a few of the many varieties; and fishermen come from all over Europe and North America to test their patience and skill at catching their supper with a rod and line. One of the most popular areas for the coarse fisherman is the River Shannon, but here his pleasure is shared with that of the boating man and the nature-lover.

The Shannon rises dramatically from a deep hole called Log Na Sionna—"The Pot"—which is an outlet for a number of underground streams and is over 150 metres (500 feet) above sea level. The whole area is mountainous, and countless tributaries and underground streams feed the river.

Flowing south-west, the Shannon is joined by the River Boyle below Hartley Bridge and it winds through the centre of Ireland. At times, the river broadens out into large lakes, such as Lough Ree and Lough Derg. When the wind gets up these loughs become covered with "white horses", like a rough sea, and they provide ample excitement and danger for the Irish who enjoy a "fair breeze" at the tiller.

The navigable inland water finishes at the southern tip of Lough Derg, at Killaloe. This is a favourite water-skiing centre and many international events are held here. Finally, the Shannon passes under an old bridge at Killaloe, and then on past Limerick to the Atlantic.

Along its 370-kilometre (230-mile) course, the River Shannon provides leisure and recreation for those who love fishing, motor-boat cruising, sailing and water-skiing. There is no close season for coarse fishing in Ireland and this makes the country all the more attractive to keen fishermen. One angling author from overseas once wrote: "Where else can you walk across a field where your right of way is not challenged? And where else will you meet a farmer who is more likely to be annoyed with you if you do *not* fish in his lake than if you do?"

The Irishmen who prefer sailing and fishing at sea keep their boats in one of the many harbours around the coast. Perhaps the most famous of these is Kinsale. From this natural harbour, fishing-smacks and catamarans go out after shark and skate. The shark is not the man-eating variety but,

Lough Derg, near Killaloe

nevertheless, it will weigh over 45 kilogrammes (about 100 lb) ;
while the skate may each weigh anything up to 90 kilogrammes (200 lb). One of the reasons why there are so
many fish in these waters is that the *Lusitania* which was
torpedoed off this coast during the First World War, now
provides first-class accommodation for many species, including giant ling, pollack, cod, conger and red bream.

At Kinsale it is also possible for a helmsman who cannot
afford his own sailing sloop to hire a four-berther and sail
round the coast—provided that he first passes a vigorous
sailing and seamanship test. At one time, in days gone by,
Kinsale was one of the chief ports of the British Navy and had

its own docks and quays where invasion craft and frigates were built. Today it is the base of yacht charterers who hire out boats for coastal sailing.

People who enjoy sailing often become keen bird-watchers, as they have constant opportunities of watching birds glide on wind currents. The Irish are no exception; many of them are amateur naturalists. A number of bird sanctuaries have therefore been established in Ireland. Bird-watchers find that in the north-east alone there are seventeen wildfowl refuges and bird observatories. Over 200 species of birds use Ireland as a breeding- or wintering-ground. They range from the brightly-coloured kingfishers to the black cormorants.

However, not all bird-watchers are content merely to study the beauty of wildlife. The woodcock is a delicacy and the shooting of it is a popular sport in Ireland during the season. Many hotels provide free shooting for their guests and offer to cook the bagged game.

Kinsale, County Cork

Peaceful beauty of the countryside

Irish game is not limited to woodcock. There is also pheasant, duck, snipe, goose and plover in the many excellent shooting-grounds—especially in the west of Ireland.

Space and freedom are part of the Irishman's way of life. He can get out of any major city into the country within half an hour and enjoy fine walks in beautiful natural surroundings. Some walks and climbs are, of course, more beautiful than others; the mountains of Connemara, for example, have inspired many famous paintings—they are among the most splendid mountain scenery in the world. Scenic grandeur, however, is never far away in Ireland. The Wicklow mountains in the east, the ring of Kerry and Dingle peninsula in the

A Connemara landscape, County Galway

south-west, the cliffs of Moher in the west, and the highlands
of Donegal in the north-west—these are just a few of the
country's natural beauty spots.

It is not surprising that Ireland, which has all the necessary
conditions for good golf, is a natural golfer's paradise. Dotted
over the country there are some 200 courses; and there are
twenty championship courses, such as Killarney, where
international events are held. Golfing in Ireland is for every-
body—since the cost of playing is relatively cheaper than in
other countries and the courses are much less crowded.

88

But Ireland's national games are not played with a golf-ball. They are hurling, Gaelic football and handball. The most exciting of all is hurling; and it is the fastest game in the world, too. It is played with hurleys (which look not unlike hockey-sticks). They are made of ash and have a broad base; this base is used to strike the small leather ball with which the game is played. The ball travels at such a speed that it is sometimes difficult for the spectators to follow its flight. To the outsider, the game is best described as a mixture of hockey and lacrosse. It is fast and dangerous and yet nearly every Irish schoolboy longs to play one day in the All-Ireland finals. For Ireland is justly renowned as a land of sport—and sportsmen.

Everything is near the water in Ireland, even some of the golf courses, like this one at Bundoran in Donegal

Ireland in the World Today

After nearly fifty years of comparative freedom from violence, Ireland again experienced civil disturbance and terrorism in the late 1960s. A movement to improve the lot of the Catholic majority in Northern Ireland eventually led to such serious rioting and killings that the British army was sent in to restore law and order to the province. The British government dissolved the Northern Ireland parliament in 1972 and Ulster is now ruled directly from Britain and sends members of parliament to sit in Westminster.

Ireland's industry is being modernised. This new factory is so near to the sea that the people who work in it can go swimming during their lunch break

A small group of people, known as the provisional IRA (Irish Republican Army), claim to be fighting for a united Ireland and they constantly harass the population and the security forces in Northern Ireland.

The government of the Irish Republic, fearful that the violence will spread over the border, has passed some very strict anti-terrorist laws. The army has been doubled in strength and soldiers patrol the border with Northern Ireland to try and prevent acts of terrorism.

In spite of these problems, the people of both Northern Ireland and the Irish Republic go about their daily business in the normal way. The economy has not suffered to any great extent in either part of the country and industrial production is competitive with that of other countries of the Western world. The Irish Republic, with its great agricultural strength, has done particularly well since 1973 when it joined the European Economic Community (the Common Market) along with Britain and Denmark.

The overwhelming majority of the people of Ireland reject the men of violence. A united Ireland may come about some day but it will not be achieved through violence. It will only happen if the hearts and minds of those who live there become united.

Index

92